The Rainbow Bee

By: Ricardo Gattas-Moras & Rob Jackson

By: Ricardo Gattas-Moras
& Rob Jackson

Library of Congress Control Number: 2021926062

Authors' Quote:

"This is a book of love and acceptance. A reminder that our differences make us beautiful and special."

Once upon a time, in a beehive far away,
a little bee was born who looked different
than any other bee that had ever been seen.
Instead of black and yellow, this bee had
stripes that were all different colors, so the
Queen decided to name the bee Rainbow.

Rainbow not only looked different, but liked different things too. Most of the hive preferred sweet nectar from garden flowers, however Rainbow's favorite was sour nectar from wild flowers.

But some bees thought Ra bow was too different to be a part of the hive, so the Queen decided to test Ra bow.

She asked to see if Rainbow could fly like the other bees. Rainbow kept up with ease! Also, positioning Rainbow at the front of the swarm made it easier for the other bees to follow along.

She asked to see if Rainbow could pollinate flowers like the other bees. Rainbow was able to pollinate perfectly, and could also pollinate the flowers with sour nectar the other bees didn't like.

She asked to see if Rainbow could buzz like
the other bees. Rainbow flew around in circles
and blissfully buzzed just like the others.

The tests made the hive realize that despite being unique and different, Rainbow still fit in great! The bees that doubted Rainbow apologized for not giving Rainbow a fair chance.

The Queen addressed the hive: "We're all a little different; Some taller, some shorter, some wider, some slimmer, some yellow and black, and some rainbow. But inside we're all the same."

"From now on, no matter what color or how different one of us is, we're going to love them all the same. Because it isn't our differences and the way we look that define us, it's how we act and treat others that determines our worth."

"Let's all remember that there is more that brings us together than separates us. So bee kind and bee open to others that are different, because loving someone is the best gift you can give to them and to yourself."

Rainbow looked up and smiled at the Queen
as the other bees gathered around to give
Rainbow hugs. From that day forward, the hive
loved and embraced one another's differences.
And Rainbow lived happily, and uniquely,
ever after.

The

End

Thank you to everyone who helped us along the way in turning this dream into a reality. A special thank you to our friends and family who have given us invaluable feedback, as well as unwavering love and support throughout this process. And most of all, thank you to our son, Cy, who's love for books at an early age inspired us to take this journey.

-Ricardo & Rob

CPSIA information can be obtained
at www.ICGtesting.com
Printed in the USA
LVHW070902160723
752311LV00049B/33